PASSING THOUGHTS

Written by
Colin Boynton

Dedicated to
Frank (Bert) Matheson – Thank You for inspiring me
And encouraging me.

ISBN : 978-0-9559931-1-4

© COLIN BOYNTON 2009

INDEX
1. HAVE YOU EVER SEEN THE DAISIES?
2. I CAN BE ANYTHING
3. THE WEALTH OF KNOWLEDGE
4. ENDANGERED SPECIES – LIFE AT RISK
5. GOODNIGHT
6. WINTERTIME
7. TRIPPING THE LIGHT FANTASTIC
8. A GIFT
9. ON THE SHORE
10. OLD FRIENDS
11. WALKIES
12. WHISPERS
13. SILENT MOVIE STARS (OR HOTEL FOYER GUESTS)
14. SOCIAL UNITY
15. SUMMER MEADOW
16. SHAME OF IT
17. NIGHT SKY LIGHT
18. LISTEN VERY CAREFULLY
19. SUMMERTIME
20. LONELY DAYS
21. SALE TIME BARGAIN
22. LAST NIGHT
23. TELEPHONE PAD
24. WHAT A DIFFERENCE A DAY MAKES
25. TORTURE – OR MUZAK TO MY EARS

26. IN LOVE WITH YOU
27. A PRAYER
28. MOONLIGHT DANCING
29. AN OLD FRIEND
30. NEXT TIME
31. RADIO DAYS
32. ONE O'CLOCK AM
33. NO GHOST AND ONE DEER
34. A QUESTION FOR YOU
35. PICTURE THIS
36. GETTING WET
37. COMMUTING
38. DAY TO DAY OR YOUNG AT HEART
39. MORE HASTE LESS SPEED
40. NOT THE TIME OR PLACE
41. THE LIGHT
42. NOW THAT SUMMER'S GONE
43. A LITTLE SECRET
44. GUILTY MAN
45. ROUTINE
46. NEVER TOO LATE
47. STAR
48. THE ANSWER IS NO!
49. ALL I HAVE TO GIVE YOU.
50. HORN OF PLENTY

51. STRANGER ON THE SHORE
52. WALK ON BY
53. STARDUST
54. CAN'T TAKE MY EYES OFF YOU
55. JUST AN OLD FASHIONED GIRL
56. WE'LL MEET AGAIN
57. THE LAST WALTZ
58. SOMEONE TO WATCH OVER ME
59. ONE VOICE
60. THEY ONLY GO OUT AT NIGHT
61. A LONG AND LASTING LOVE
62. THE WORLD TODAY
63. GHOSTS
64. CRAZY OR NOT
65. WHY QUESTION…
66. THE NEWS
67. REMEMBERING VERA LYNN
68. MOTORWAY
69. IT'S A SIN
70. A PRAYER
71. ANOTHER ENDING, ANOTHER GOODBYE
72. MOTHER
73. FATHER
74. NATURES PICTURE
75. MY PRIVATE PLACE

76. OLD AGE BIRTHDAY
77. BIRD OF PREY
78. RETIREMENT PLAN
79. MR PEACEMAKER
80. THE GOOD AND THE BAD
81. WHY
82. FRIENDSHIP
83. ONE, TWO, THREE, ONE, TWO, THREE
84. TUNISIA
85. PROMENADE DAYS
86. THE OLD SONGS
87. WHO'S NEXT?
88. AUTUMN
89. PLEASE YOURSELF
90. PASSING PEOPLE
91. TOGETHER – YOU AND ME
92. TRUE LOVE
93. ALL I HAVE TO GIVE YOU
94. SHARING
95. THOUGHTS FROM A TRAVEL COURIER
96. 'TIS THE SEASON TO BE JOLLY
97. CHRISTMAS
98. BECAUSE OF YOU
99. YOU'LL NEVER WALK ALONE
100.   THE DOLLY SISTERS

1. HAVE YOU EVER SEEN THE DAISIES ?

Have you ever seen the daisies
Blooming in the grass,
Or to you are they just a nuisance
Growing there en mass?
Do you ever take the time
To stop and smell a rose,
Do you ever ask yourself
And wonder how it grows?
Do you ever see the old men
Walking down the street,
Or do you cross on over
Hoping you don't meet?
Do these things annoy you
Embarrass you as well,
And yet the world's in turmoil
And on the road to hell.
Will anybody stop it,
Can anybody see,
The way to make a better world
Fit for you and me.
Don't ignore the simple things
Don't ignore the old,
And don't ignore what's happening
All around the world.

2. I CAN BE ANYTHING

I can be anything
I can be rich
Grow up a flower
Or grow up a witch
I can fly high
Up above trees
Or swim with the fishes
Deep in the seas
I can be superman
I'll save the world
But I can be quiet
And do as I'm told
Now I'm invisible
You cannot see me
Running around
As fast as can be
I can do anything
Cause I'm Johnny – I'm five
And when I'm at infant's school
I come alive,

(I'm also a little horror, so says my Mum)

3. THE WEALTH OF KNOWLEDGE

Yesterday, tomorrow seemed
A long, long way away
And now the years have rushed on by
Tomorrow is today.
Yesterday is now long gone
A far off memory
But still I can but wonder
What the future holds for me.
I used to dream of what I'd do
The places I might go
And now that I have done these things
I still don't even know.
Will I grow old gracefully,
Keep my pride, my health,
Could I still be happy,
With all this untold wealth?

4. ENDANGERED SPECIES – LIFE AT RISK

You steal our homes
And move us on
You don't seem happy
'Til they're gone,
You kill our friends
One by one
Yet call yourselves
"Fellow Man"
So what gives you?
The solemn right
To take away
Our chance of life,
Nature's meant
For all to share
But most of you
Don't seem to care
So go on, kill us
One by one
We won't be missed
Until we're gone.

5. GOODNIGHT

The world keeps slowly turning round
Time keeps ticking by
Older now, and wiser now
Just my friend and I.
The fireside glow
May warm our feet
On long cold winter nights
Valley sides and meadows
Our favourite summer sights.
No longer can we run around
Age has made its toll
And still there remains
Our same old cheery souls.
We may not see as many friends
So many have gone on
I know you won't dessert me
You've loved me true and long.
And as I wait here to retire
I watch the embers die
You wag your tail contentedly
And look me in the eye.
So lift our feet so wearily
Make our way to bed
We'll close our eyes for one last night
And rest our weary heads.

6. WINTERTIME

In the middle of the winter
While snow lay on the ground
Snow that lay so soft and deep
No footsteps made a sound.
The sky it looked so dark and grim
With clouds so very grey
It made it seem like night time
In the middle of the day.
Cold crept round each corner
From winter winds that howl
Hunting out its victims
Like a wolf that's on the prowl.
Whipped into a frenzy
Snow that falls so quiet
Drifts up by the hedge sides
In the middle of the night.
Changing views and changing scenes
Hiding things from view
And nowhere, nothing looks the same
Everything looks new.
In the middle of the winter
While snow lay on the ground
Nothing moved, nothing stirred
Nothing made a sound.

7. TRIPPING THE LIGHT FANTASTIC

Old Miss Flo was a merry old soul
Went out every Wednesday lunch,
With her glad rags on and a heart full of song
She hopped on a number 9 bus.
Once in town she walked around
Killing time for an hour or so,
Then down to the Palais this lady wouldn't dally
For the afternoon tea and dance.
Tripping the light fantastic
Stepping on her partners toes
Every week, the same routine
And soon it began to show.
Old Miss Flo still loved to go
Dancing every week
But two months on she had no one
Who would dance, who could dance with her.
Feet black and blue from you know who
Pour soul didn't mean no harm
Now six months on she still goes on
She dances all alone.
Tripping the light fantastic
No feet to tread upon
Dear Miss Flo will not be stopped
She just goes on and on.

8. A GIFT

If you've ever seen sunshine on water
Or moonlight on glistening frost,
Heard rustling leaves
Or the buzzing of bees
Do you know how it feels to be lost…
In a scene full of beauty,
A world full of charm
Where birds can fly high
And the winds rush on by
Do you know how it feels to be warm…
In your heart that is lifted
And feel that the gift is
Given to all and to you
Keep sight of these things
And whatever life brings
Your spirit will lift when it's down.

9. ON THE SHORE

Sandy beaches, sunny days
Nought to do but sit and laze
Air is stirred by whispered breeze
On the shores of foreign seas.

Water washing over feet
The beach is busy like a street
People going everywhere
Coming up to sell their ware
Where sun is cooled by whispered breeze
On the shores of foreign seas.

And even when the sun is low
It's still a place where people go,
And while the moon reflects its light
They gaze with awe upon this sight
Whilst all's made cooler by the breeze
On the shores of foreign seas.

10. OLD FRIENDS

Step back in time with me my friend
Step back in time with me
There's the field where once we played
And this our favourite tree.
Through fallen leaves we'd kick our way
Let's do it once just now,
Played games in the old schoolyard
Come let me show you how.
Remember German measles?
You caught that from me,
We skipped, we ran, we shouted
Fell and grazed a knee.
We had a gang, we had a den
Built high up in a tree
That old familiar voice of mother
Called us for our tea.
Step back in time with me my friend
Wander memory lane
Whatever things I used to do
I guess you did the same.

11. WALKIES

Left foot, right foot, pause
Urban, rural walks
Left foot, right foot, paws
Master even talks.
We like to go out roving
Together every day
I take him for his walkies
We like it much that way.
The only thing I find
A problem (small I add)
I like the weather good
Don't like it when it's bad.
We go out many times a day
We don't go all that far,
But sometimes on a weekend
We'll go out in the car.
I'm happy with the life I lead
As you can plainly see,
I wouldn't change a single thing
"A doggy's life's for me!"

12. WHISPERS

A whisper passes
By my ears
Almost silent
No one hears
A gentle sound
Among the trees
The whisper of
An evening breeze.

13. SILENT MOVIE STARS (OR HOTEL FOYER GUESTS)

As I sit here watching
I wonder "Do they know?"
The world is slowly passing by
A silent picture show.
Coming in from nowhere
Going to the same,
Some faces tell a story
Yet none will have a name.
Each person is an actor
Acting out life's play
Innocently taking part,
They do it every day.
So as I sit here watching
I wonder if they know
That each and every one of them
Is in my picture show.

14. SOCIAL UNITY

Everybody has one
Not are all the same
Some are big, others small
Yet go by just one name.
Some of them will seem to glow
Others are less bright,
All can shine in daylight hours
And even in the night.
Something that can ease the fears
Join the lonely few,
Doesn't cost a thing
And very harmless too.
What's this international thing
That spans a many mile –
The thing we have in common
Something called a smile.

15. SUMMER MEADOW

Yellow, white
Green and blue
Every shade and every hue
No set pattern
No set way
Growing slowly day by day
Getting taller
Growing strong
Blessed by sun and sweet bird song
No disturbance
Just a breeze
Drifting on into the trees
Yellow, white
Green and blue
Sometimes red and orange too !

16. SHAME OF IT

Many are the varied tales
To you I could tell,
Stories from the years gone by
Of people I knew well.
Some have been and stayed a while
Others stayed for years
Some of them seemed friendly
Others had their fears.
They never understand it
When I come around
I try to move so peacefully
Without the faintest sound.
I think that some have seen me,
Others have just guessed
And there's nothing they can really do
With uninvited guests.
I really cannot help it
You know I'm not to blame
I didn't ask to be a spook
It really is a shame.

17. NIGHT SKY LIGHT

There's a full moon peeping
Through a cloud passing by,
Surrounded by the twinkling
Of stars in the sky.
Set in deep black
On the darkest of nights,
Now all aglow
From these wonderful lights.

18. LISTEN VERY CAREFULLY

We ran so fast
And jumped so high
We never heard
The warning cry.

So now we have
To pay the price
We never heard
The good advice.

We kept on rushing
At great speed
We never heard
We had no need.

And now it's almost
Far too late
We'll never hear
About our fate.

19. SUMMERTIME

Those long hot days of summer
Of years that seem long gone
We always will remember
And memories linger on.
The sweetest smell of new mown hay,
The sound of humming bees,
Butterflies once fluttered by
Birds flew above the trees.
The sky seemed so much bluer then
Clouds so far and few,
Long, warm, lazy evenings
Soon day would start anew.
Each one seemed much brighter
Longer, calmer, still,
Everyone was happy then
Perhaps they always will,
In long hot days of summer
For many years to come
Always be remembering
As memories linger on.

20. LONELY DAYS

Have you seen the old man
Who stands down by the sea?
He goes there almost every day
What does he go to see?
Sometimes a tear may fill his eyes,
A memory full of pain,
In the summer sunshine
Or in the winter rain.
A solitary figure
Standing all alone,
No one there beside him
Or waiting back at home.
It only seems like yesterday
That sad and fateful day,
After loving all those years
His wife had passed away.
No chance to say a last farewell
It happened far too fast,
No time to give one last fond kiss
Too soon her life had passed.
Now he goes down to the shore
Looking out to sea,
There's nothing much left these days
But a special memory.
And sometimes that eludes him
And then the tears will start,
Why must he now be punished
With this painful broken heart.
A family all gone now
His friends all passed away,
All alone now in this world
He still comes every day.
What did he do that was so wrong
To earn him so much pain,
He only ever gave his love
That cannot come again.
An old and lonely figure
Stands down by the sea,
And sometime in the future
That old man could be me.

21. SALE TIME BARGAIN

I bought myself a thingy
But don't know what it's for,
It really looked quite useful
As it lay there on the floor.
He only wanted four pounds
And so I offered three,
I'm now the proud possessor
Of a "What can this thing be?"
It really was a bargain
To be sold as cheap as that,
But is it really useful
Or just a piece of tat?
I'm not sure where I'll put it
It might go on a shelf,
Standing with some other things
Or standing by itself.
Perhaps one day I'll find out
Just what this thing can be,
Until that day upon the shelf
I'll leave my bargain thingy.

22. LAST NIGHT (Pt 1)

I woke up from a dream last night
The monster wasn't there,
Six foot tall, eyes of black
It looked just like a teddy bear.
I closed my eyes and settled down
Once more began to snore,
I woke up from the dream again
Was that the bedroom door?
I lay awake and listened
But couldn't hear a sound,
Silently I left my bed
To have a look around.
Accepting there was nothing there
I made my way to bed,
And feeling very tired now
I soon lay down my head

LAST NIGHT (Pt 2)

I woke up from a dream again
Or had I been asleep?
I'm sure that something moved about
Dare I take a peep?
Six feet tall, eyes of black
The biggest hands you've ever seen
Seemingly searching around
Would I go unseen?
I held my breath the best I could
And hoped it wouldn't see
For if this monster realised
Would it let me be?
Gingerly I slipped right down
The bed clothes hid me well
Would this monster go away?
I really couldn't tell.

LAST NIGHT (Pt 3)

I found I couldn't dream no more
But wished I really could,
Whatever moved around the room
Frightened me real good.
I wished it wouldn't stay there
I wanted it to go
And my stupid curiosity
Felt a need to know.
Six feet tall, eyes of black
With hair as white as snow
Slinging something on its back
It made the move to go.
I woke up from a dream last night
Feeling rather restless,
Aged forty eight I now believe
There is a Father Christmas!

23. TELEPHONE PAD

Circles, squares and diamonds
Squiggles, numbers too,
The strangest things on telephone pads
People find to do.
Half a message left last week
Reminders for the day,
Written down in short hand
Or some annotated way.
When looked at in the future
It doesn't make much sense,
Why Aunty Jo was eating
Next doors garden fence!

24. WHAT A DIFFERENCE A DAY MAKES

The postman passed by again today
No one rang, with nothing to say.
Someone called round, I wasn't in
The pools came up, I didn't win.
A pan boiled over, the kettle boiled dry
Call this a day, I could just sit and cry.
Instead of tears falling, I just sit and laugh
And hear water rush from my overflowed bath.
It's not even noon, nothings gone right
Perhaps I should just hide away out of sight.
A lunchtime snooze, an afternoon nap
Awakened to find something laid in my lap.
Where did it come from, how'd it get in?
A very strange cat washing its chin.
It's eaten my dinner, the fish isn't there,
I've nought else to eat, the cupboard is bare.
It's now half past eight, what will I do?
Make a big pot of pussycat stew?
Pussycat stew, what an idea,
But I'd get indigestion from that, I fear…
Please be to God let's go to bed
Anything more and I'll go bang my head.
The blankets been on the bed should be warm,
My goodness it's freezing, the fuse must have blown.
Tossing and turning, awake all the night,
The postman called by at the first break of light.
"A letter to sign for, a beautiful day,
My but you're grumpy, what did I say?"

25. TORTURE – OR MUZAK TO MY EARS?

Muzak, muzak, muzak
All I seem to hear
Everywhere I seem to go
It pounds into my ear.
You cannot quite distinguish
What tune it is they play
And worse, it seems to drone right through
Each hour of the day.
You cannot quite escape it
It follows you around,
From shop to shop, lift to lift
You hear that dreadful sound.
Created just to torment?
Or drive a poor soul mad?
The worst of human tortures
A person ever had.

26. IN LOVE WITH YOU…

Two hearts that beat as one
Never mind the rain
And stars they find to wish upon
Will always hide the pain.
Together on a seashore,
Entwined beneath the sun,
A single lonely moonbeam lights
Two hearts that beat as one.

27. A PRAYER

When I'm feeling down and low
It feels like no one's there
Lift me up and carry me
My soul's as light as air.
Comfort me and guide me
Show me where to go
I guess you are the only one
Who really seems to know.
And when my heart is heavy
And life seems hard to bear
I take a look around me
And know you really care.

28. MOONLIGHT DANCING

A dimming light and fiery glow
With daylight hours fading slow,
A changing scene and different view
Walking hand in hand with you.
A fleeting cloud in starlit skies,
The distant shrill of night bird cries,
Rustling leaves blown by the winds,
My moonlight dance with you begins.

Shadows cast a perfect dance
Moonlight thrown, down by chance,
Waltzing round, dancing slow
They're moonlight dancing in the snow,
Moonlight dancing slow with you
Through dreamlike spires draped with dew,
Moonlight dancing you and I
'Til night time clouds fill the sky,
Then once again we'll make our way
Two in love at break of day.

29. AN OLD FRIEND

It might be slightly battered
Looking rather worn
The colours may be fading
On the covers that are torn.
It holds for me fond memories
Of sitting by the fire
Listening to some music
Or just the piece and quiet.
It still is very comfy
With room to curl and sleep
Who cares what age or state it's in
My favourite chair I'll keep.

30. NEXT TIME

Sitting by the fireside
The lights are turned down low
And once again the thought occurs
"Where did the years all go?"
A tear may fall, a smile break out
While thinking of what's gone
The memories keep on coming through
Slowly one by one.
Suddenly the silence breaks
A clock begins to chime
The memories are chased away
Until another time.

31. RADIO DAYS

Grandma's in her rocking chair
Needles in her hands
Baby booties growing
While she listens to the bands.
The radio keeps playing
Tunes from long ago
Bringing back the memories
A tear begins to show.
The unexpected playing-
A favourite melody
Played for Grandma in her chair
From son and family.

32. ONE O'CLOCK A.M.

What's that noise I'm hearing
It seems to be near by
Nocturnal sounds of creatures
Do they crawl or do they fly?
It sounded like a gurgle,
I know it didn't squeak
With sounds like that around at night
I know I will not sleep.
There goes another gurgle
That sound I've grown to hate,
But hark! – it is my stomach
From something that I ate.

33. NO GHOST AND ONE DEER

On the road into Lochinver
In the early evening light
Everything is still
There's not a car in sight.
Houses distanced far apart
Is anyone at home?
Some look quite deserted
Standing all alone.
A wild and windswept landscape
Sweeps down from the sky,
Falling into loch and stream
And waters passing by.
Trees are silhouetted
On a canvas dull and grey
Of clouds that have descended
At the closing of the day.
Is that the ghost of old McD?
Does he wander here?
But as I take a second look
I see a lonely deer.

34. A QUESTION FOR YOU…

How many more men have to die
Before we ask the question why ?
What they do, what is it for
Fighting – killing – destruction – war !
When will peace be seen again
How long will this evil reign
Are we just too blind to see
And just too deaf and let it be
Can't we rise with one loud voice
Or have we simply got no choice
How many more men have to die
And grieving families have to cry ?

35. PICTURE THIS

Framed by summer sunshine
Or lit by evening sun
A picture hangs before you
To be viewed by anyone
The artwork is superb
The detail is supreme
The colours are the brightest
I think I've ever seen
The picture is immaculate
The scene, it is divine
That's how I view the countryside
Each and every time.

36. GETTING WET

Down by the duck pond
At the bottom of the park,
I saw someone go rushing by
And heard a big dog bark.
I'd seen a flash of fur go by
Just before the dash
And shortly after seeing them
I heard a great loud splash.
Peeping from behind a bush
There all soaking wet
I saw a man sat in the pond
Holding to his pet.
I saw a cat sat on the fence
Looking down with glee
At a man and his dog
As wet as they could be.
The man looked very angry
The dog was now in shame
The cat they'd chased right through the park
Had done it once again.

37. COMMUTING

An endless stream of traffic
Heading into town
With every kind of worker
From builders to a clown.
Women putting make up on
Men on mobile phones
Asking if their wives can bring
Things they left at home
Early morning rush hour
Always is the same
Dodging round the traffic
Changing lane to lane.
This madness happens once again
When five o'clock comes around
And all these tired workers
Are driving homeward bound.

38. DAY TO DAY OR YOUNG AT HEART

Yesterday
- I felt like dancing
Today
- I'd like to run
Tomorrow
- Well who knows
I'll wait for it to come.

Last week
- I felt like walking
Next week
- I'm in the sun
I like to keep on doing
The things I've always done.
So-
- I'll live my life
From day to day
The only way I can
I suppose one really should do
Once they're eighty one!

39. MORE HASTE LESS SPEED

I walked along the riverside
And fed some ducks some bread,
I felt the rain was starting
As it fell upon my head.
I didn't want to get too wet
I had no coat or hat,
And so I started running
To where my car was at.
But as I ran much faster
My feet began to slip,
I fell into the river
And felt such a drip,
For if I'd walked much slower
I would not now be wet
The rain had passed on over,
So that is what you get,
If you rush at what you do
You'll only get some pain,
You'll make mistakes along the way
And have to start again!

40. NOT THE TIME OR PLACE

Alarm clock rings at half past five
I leave my bed, feel half alive,
My eyes still shut, my brain asleep
I feel so tired, I could just weep.
I eat my breakfast, drink my tea
With eyes half shut, I cannot see
The minutes ticking, hours by,
The sun now shining in the sky.
Feeling late I grab my things
On going out the phone then rings,
I run back in pick up the phone,
To find the caller had now gone.
I run back out, jump in the car
And not before I get too far,
I turn the radio to play
And then a voice begins to say,
"Take it easy, take it slow
It's time to start the Sunday Show"
No longer tired but wide awake
I put my foot upon the brake,
Feeling stupid, what to say
Don't have to go to work today!

41. THE LIGHT

Competing with each other
In the dark expanse of night
Shining in the darkness
Are different kinds of light.
The romance that is moonlight,
The romance of a star
Shining in the heavens
A light that travels far
The flickering candle light
And fire embers glow
A winter night made brighter
By reflections on the snow.
Looked at from a distance
The wide expanse of light
A city never seems to sleep
Through darkness of night.
And all of them keep shining
A glowing in the dark
From stars out in the heavens
To the smallest spark.

42. NOW THAT SUMMER'S GONE

Now that summer's over
And days have grown quite cold,
The trees are looking weary
Now they're growing old.
The birds have started gathering
All have flown away
And nights are so much longer
Making shorter day.
The frost is on the ground now,
The ground is hard and white
The first snow fall of winter
Will soon hide all from sight.
Winter feels so cold and harsh
The months seem very long,
As we're getting older
Now that summer's gone.

43. A LITTLE SECRET

She stands there by the roadside
The same time every day
Watching people passing by
Going on their way.
Her world is in some plastic bags
She keeps them by her side
And never bothers anyone
From morning 'til eventide.
And in the long dark night time hours
She settles down to rest,
Shelt'rin from the winds and rain
Wherever is the best.
She has no home, no money,
No friends, no family too,
And yet she's always cheerful
Why? I wish I knew.
And if I knew her secret
Why she wears a smile,
My life might be much better
If only for a while.

Guilty Man (Cont.)

I looked at her in horror
I guess she didn't see
By helping her in this way
She made me feel guilty.
But once again she begged me
"Just let me one more time"
And so I finally gave in
Agreed to her small crime.
What is it with this woman
I call my dear old gran?
Makes me do these silly things,
And I'm the guilty man.
Living in the way she does
In this old folks home,
She only wants to get out
And have a little roam.
And every time I help her
And give a little chance,
She goes off to the Palaise
Where she likes to dance,
And cause it really does no harm
I help her all I can,
She's a happy lady
I'm still a guilty man!

44. GUILTY MAN

Slipping out the back door
Quietly at night,
Creeping through the shadows
Keeping hid from sight.
If anyone should notice
Or anyone should see,
Then all my days of planning
Would be a waste for me.
I know I shouldn't do it
But what else could I do?
She begged and begged for days on end
And then I gave in too,
She told me all her reasons
We argued wrong from right,
Until I finally gave in
And fixed this fateful night.
Provided no one noticed
And all went as to plan,
The night would be successful
But I'm a guilty man.
I didn't hear for days on end
I guessed that all went well,
And so I went to visit
She had her tale to tell.
The smile she had upon her face
That day as I walked in,
Told me all had gone well
And "Could she go again?"
……cont

45. ROUTINE

At the same time every morning
At the same place every day
Are the same familiar faces
Going on their way.
Going through the motions
No thought to what they do
Their lives are getting boring
And getting tiresome too.
They look for some excitement
There's nothing to be found
Just the same old dull routine
On just the same old ground.
And then one day it happens
A bolt from out the blue
Does anybody notice
Or know just what to do.
Because the routine's boring
We never really see
Just how interesting
Life can really be.

46. NEVER TOO LATE

Sit down here beside me Dad
There's something I must say
It's been upon my mind now
For many a long day.
These words do not come easy
What I must tell you now
Although it's very simple
I'm not sure yet just how.
For years you've helped me in my life
You showed me right from wrong
And when I needed your support
You were always strong.
I've taken you for granted
You've always been around
You've always come to rescue me
Without a single sound.
And now as we grow older
There's something I must do
I want to give my heartfelt thanks
And say Dad "I love you"

47. STAR

A little light is shining
Almost out of view
It's been there for a long time now
You must have seen it too.
It's shining in the distance
The light must travel far
Coming through the night sky
From a tiny star.

48. THE ANSWER IS NO!

What would I do – if you weren't here?
How could I live – without you near?
You put the smile
Upon my face
You lift me up
With just one kiss.
Who would I dream of – when I'm asleep?
Who'd dry my tears – whenever I weep?
Who would I cuddle?
Who'd I caress?
Where would I be
With no one to bless?
With no one to wish me – a very goodnight
Or wish me good morning – at first break of light
Could I be strong?
Or could I be bold?
If you weren't here
For me to hold.

49. ALL I HAVE TO GIVE YOU

All I have to give you
Is a little of my love
I cannot give you falling stars
Or the moon above.
I'll lay my life before you
My heart, my soul, my all
I'll always be around for you
Just in case you fall.
And if my little piece of love
Is just enough for you
Take it gently in your heart
To last your whole life through.

50. HORN OF PLENTY

Nose to tail
In single file
A hot and sultry day
Patience slowly growing thin
And tempers start to fray.
A single honk from far behind
Or somewhere way in front?
Nothing moved for half an hour
Not a single shunt.
The noise soon grows much louder
(As more patience snaps)
From cars and drivers caught up in
Holiday road works traps.

51. STRANGER ON THE SHORE

Footsteps in the wet sand
Led me ever on
Past the rocks and seaweed
In the evening sun.
The gentle lapping on the shore
Creeping ever near
And still I followed onward
The footsteps with no fear.
A gentle breeze caressed my brow
I slowly strolled along
The sea was washing on my feet
The footsteps soon were gone.
I stopped to look behind me
And then I looked ahead
I saw the footsteps rising
A voice behind me said,
"Following my footsteps
You know you won't go wrong,
Follow in my footsteps
To grow forever strong."
I turned around to face
My stranger on the shore
The one who'd made those footsteps
Was standing there no more.
I turned and started following
Footsteps in the sand
Until the sun was setting
Behind my very land.
I lay me down upon the shore
And then I closed my eyes
Then when I looked about me
The stars were in the skies.

52. WALK ON BY

You pass them by most every day
The old folk in the street
And then you see that someone
You didn't want to meet.
Face to face and eye to eye
Withered now with age,
Walking oh so slowly
Your heart is filled with rage.
No one seems to notice
Does anybody care?
They pass by very quickly
As if he wasn't there.
Just one smile is all it takes
Not money or your wealth,
Remember that in years to come
You will get old yourself.

53. STARDUST

A blanket of moonbeams
Covers the land
As two young lovers
Walk hand in hand
Down quiet country lanes
They're strolling along
And listening to
The night birds song.

High in the heavens
Way up above
These two young people
So much in love
Stars begin twinkling
One by one
The last of the day
Now finally gone.

The night air still
And feeling cold
Encompass the lovers
Now grown old
But still they stroll
Down country lanes
Their stardust memories
Still remains.

54. CAN'T TAKE MY EYES OFF YOU

I Know I've seen you here before
And time and time again
I've watched you passing slowly by
And once more felt the pain.
The pain of knowing what I know
Of things I cannot hold
I know that I must wear a smile
Appear that I am bold.
Yet every time I see you
I find I stop and stare
And still you always pass me by
As if I wasn't there.
Could anybody tell me
What I need to do
To make you stop and notice me
And know my love is true.
I know that you're with someone else
So what am I to do?
Trapped here in this dog's home
In need of one like you.

55. JUST AN OLD FASHIONED GIRL

Call me old fashioned
I don't care,
Things are not
The way they were
Things have changed
Time's moved on
The good old days
Have finally gone.

So don't tell me
You don't care
That things are not
The way they were
Even we
Have had to change
Which seems to be
A little strange.

I really think
We ought to care
When things are not
The way they were
Let's get back
The things we had
'Cause life without them
Seems quite sad.

I'm old fashioned
But I don't care
I'd still like things
The way they were
How they were
When I was young
Before the world
Was highly strung.

56. WE'LL MEET AGAIN ((apologies to) VERA LYNN)

Eskimo Nell, her Mum and her Dad
Sat down on Christmas Day
Greeted by the wonderful smell
Of cooking drifting their way.
They sucked their white wine ice cubes
Crunched their nuts from May
Looked forward to the wonderful meal
About to come their way.

The days and weeks soon passed by
With leftovers much the same
Casseroles, stews and sandwiches
Repeats with a different name
And finally November came around
Nell was heard to complain
"Oh Mum, not more of that leftover
Whale meat again!"

57. THE LAST WALTZ

I'll never be a singer
Or a dancer in a show,
The noise that comes from out my mouth
Would make the people go.
With two left feet to trip upon
I really must confess
When I get out on the floor
I look a total mess.
I'll never play an instrument
Or write a well read book,
I think that I must be tone deaf
Making people look.
With pen in hand I try to write
But words just seem to fail
With nothing written on the page
I cannot tell a tale.
I'll never be a singer
Or a dancer in a show,
But can we have the last dance
Before I have to go.
I will not step upon your feet
I promise that to you,
So can I have the last waltz
It's all that I can do.

58. SOMEONE TO WATCH OVER ME

There it goes again
I saw the curtain move
She's peeping out once more on us
It only goes to prove
She could be just plain nosey
And doesn't really care
If we see the curtain twitch
And know that she is there.
Can we ever leave the house
Without being seen?
She's watching over you and me
And anyone who's been
It could be that she's lonely
With nowhere else to be
Or could it be in secret
She really fancies me.

59. ONE VOICE

I listen to the rhythm
Of my beating heart
Telling me about the things
I knew right from the start.
Like just how much I love you
And what you mean to me
And every little thing we've shared
And how great life can be
I've listened to no other
Since you came along
With just one voice you've shown me
Together we belong.

60. THEY ONLY GO OUT AT NIGHT

She lived alone down by the sea
In a cottage built for two,
What she did there every day
Nobody ever knew.
And every day she'd stay inside
Keeping out of sight,
The only time she ventured out
Was in the dark of night.
No one came and no one went
She stayed there all alone,
You couldn't see her garden path
For it was over grown.
Ivy grew up on the roof
And all around each wall,
You couldn't see the windows
Summer, spring or fall.
And in the dark of winter
When snow lay on the ground,
She still stay hidden out of sight
And never made a sound.
No one ever knew how old she was
And no one seemed to care,
And though they never saw her
They knew that she was there.
Why no one ever bothered
No body ever said,
But everybody knew she was
One of the living dead.
And vampires stay inside each day
For them day isn't good,
They only venture out at night
When looking for some blood!

61. A LONG AND LASTING LOVE.

Someone sits alone tonight
And cries a tear or two
Feeling lost and lonely
Not knowing what to do.
Someone else is left alone
To live without their love
Sitting looking at the stars
In the sky above.
Thinking of tomorrow
In dreams of yesterday
Watching other people
Not knowing what to say.
And as each hour passes by
They slowly realise
The love that they have always had
Never, ever dies.

62. THE WORLD TODAY

What is the world all about
Why do we go on killing?
Why can't we live together in peace
Instead of the blood we keep spilling?
Most of the time we may never have met
Until we are eye to eye
And then without anyone starting to speak
Somebody happens to die.
Be it by bullet or be it by bomb
Or even be it by knife
There's hatred inside you cannot explain
That makes someone take a life.
Why can't we live together in peace
And just let each other be?
The world could be a better place
For people like you and me.

63. GHOSTS

Paying no attention
In the corner of my eye
The shadow of a figure
Slowly passing by.
Turning round to take a look
There's no one standing by
It's just the shadow of a ghost
Which seems to catch my eye.

I hear the sound of laughter
Ringing in my ear
A sound so real I turn to look
There's no one standing near.
And yet it sounded very real
The laughter I could hear
The ghost of someone from my past
Sounding loud and clear.

64. CRAZY OR NOT

If nobody ever told me
And nobody ever said
I'm sure by now I would have heard
From the voices in my head.
Some people think I'm crazy
Others say I'm mad
But the voices I hear in my head
Say they are just being bad.
They say I should be locked away
Safely in a home
But the voices that I hear in my head
Say that I should roam.
I know that I'm not crazy
Just because I said
I listen what the voices say
Going round my head.

65. WHY QUESTION…

Why question the reason
A bird has to fly
Or why the clouds
Are up in the sky.
Why question the reason
A tree has to grow
Or what makes a river
Continue to flow.
Why question the reason
The stars shine at night
Or why the moon
Still shines so bright.
Why ask these questions
And so many more
When we don't even know
What our own lives are for.
Why question the beauty
Of all that we see
When we haven't yet learnt
To let these things be.

66. THE NEWS.

Yesterday I heard the news
It made me want to cry
Someone's out there suffering
Another child will die
With bombs and guns we aim to kill
Creating misery
And someone else is crying out
Will we ever see
A way to end the hatred
A way to end the fear
Or will we go on hurting
And shed another tear.
What's the point in killing
Just for killings sake
Can we ever stop it?
How long will it take?

67. REMEMBERING VERA LYNN.

There was to be –
Bluebirds over
The white cliffs of Dover
We just had to wait and see.
We were to have –
Love and laughter
And peace ever after
How wrong could they ever be?
All of those lives
Those husbands and wives
Their sons and their daughters too,
All of those years
And all of those tears
If only our heroes knew.
Now there's nothing flies over
Those white cliffs of Dover
We fear what the future might bring,
And the love that we had
Like the peace, has turned bad
You can't even hear what they sing.
It's sad when they say
"Not like yesterday."
When their lives are nearly over
But they still like to hear
Year after year
Vera sing "White Cliffs Of Dover"

68. MOTORWAY.

Junction one, junction two
Junction three, junction four
Motorway miles can be such a bore,
Car after car, bus after bus
And slow moving lorries making me cuss,
A biker in leathers is riding the storm
You think yourself lucky, that you're dry and warm
The sun comes out, you're happy again
There's nothing worse, than driving in rain
With nothing to see but the traffic ahead
If you don't watch it well –
You might well end up dead!

69. IT'S A SIN!

It's always hard work being death
Working night and day
Forever always on the go
For very little pay.
Sometimes it is a struggle
When your client won't sit still
The job is so much easier
When they're very ill
It really can get tiring
Working night and day
No time to get a weekend off
Or take a holiday
And people seem ungrateful
With the things you do
But I don't want to do this job
If only people knew
It's passed on down the family line
And I was next one in
You see, I trained to be a fairy
It really is a sin!

70. A PRAYER.

Thank you Lord
For one more day
For giving me
The chance to say
Thank you for
The things you've done
I'll count my blessings
One by one.

71. ANOTHER ENDING, ANOTHER GOODBYE.

The first leaves turned to gold
Curled about,
Then fell,
The days became much shorter
Cold and dark
As well,
Nature slowly fell asleep
Winter days
Crept on
Only brightened now and then
With glimpses of
A winter sun.
The winter winds
Blew hard
Blew strong
And frosty nights
Seemed cold
Seemed long
The ending of another day
Another week
A year
A time to say goodbye once more
To many things held dear.

72. MOTHER

A friend who is special
Someone to care
Whenever you need her
You know she'll be there.
Joining your laughter
Easing your pain
Always around
Through sunshine and rain
Someone to cherish
Hold dear to your heart
You know that she's loved you
Right from the start.

And now that I'm older
Stronger and wise
I still see the love
In my Mothers eyes.

73. FATHER.

Fathers never seem around
And yet they're always there,
Giving you the love you need
Showing that they care.
A strong and firm, yet gentle hand
Guiding you along,
Helping make your dreams come true,
Building you a home.
Working hard throughout the day
Working to provide
Thinking of the family
A gentleman of pride.
Although there may seem distance
In between our hearts
I know you'll always love me
And never let us part.
So in return for all you've done
And what you've given me
I want to give my love to you,
I want the world to see
The special kind of man you are
And all you mean to me,
No one could replace you
The best a Dad could be.

74. NATURES PICTURE.

The sun comes up
And day begins
The sky is reigned
By birds on wings
No cloud to greet
The morning view
No frosty chill
Or early dew.
A hazy scene
Might greet the eye
A sign that good things
Should pass by.
A hum and buzz
A flower quiver
'Tis the bumble
Cause this shiver.
Sky of blue
Grass that's green
Multi hued flowers
Crowd the scene.
All a part
Each one a piece
Of this picture each eye sees.
Radiant light
Reflects the glory
Of each colour
In the story,
Of each day
That passes by
Created for
Our humble eye.

75. MY PRIVATE PLACE (OF PEACE AND SERENITY)

A swirling mass of colour
On a bright and sunny day
A gentle breeze to sail on through
And make the colours sway.
Towering high above the grass
Beneath a sky of blue
Reaching out across the land
To make a perfect view.
Flowers in a meadow
A meadow small and bright
Waiting there for all to see
Yet hidden out of sight.

76. OLD AGE BIRTHDAY.

Another golden autumn
Another summer gone
Winter's soon upon us
With days so cold and long.
Another year to celebrate
But many friends have gone
The family has grown up
They too have moved along.
Few can now remember
Each birthday that comes round
Age don't seem to matter
That's one thing I have found.
But someone does remember
I see the dark clouds part
The sun peeps through and shines on down
To warm an old mans heart.

77. BIRD OF PREY.

The morning sun
Glints upon
The wings of birds of prey,
Gliding by
Across the sky
At the break of day.
Traveling to a far land
Or from shores so far away
Flying many miles and hours
A graceful bird today
The airplane is really just
A giant bird of prey
Feeding on the people
Who need to get away.

78. RETIREMENT PLAN

Feeling down and feeling glum
Now your working days are done
So now you're older and more wise
Try to see it through my eyes.
I've got to get up every day
Rain or snow come what may,
I've got to make things move along
Even when I'm not that strong.
I can't just down tools walk away
And take an unplanned holiday,
Weary? Tired? Need a rest?
But I still have to do my best.
Earn a penny, earn a pound
The working day soon comes around,
Gosh, that makes me feel quite glum
I wish my working life was done.

79. MR PEACEMAKER.

Hey, Mr Peacemaker
What's gone wrong?
I don't hear you sing your song
I don't see you round here no more
You've closed your windows, locked your door
Don't you hear your people shout?
Don't you want to sort things out?

Hey. Mr Peacemaker
Where are you?
What are we supposed to do?
We do not listen, do not hear
Now we live our lives in fear
Don't you hear us pray each night?
Don't you want to put things right?

Hey, Mr Peacemaker
Do you see?
Is this how it's meant to be?
Is this how we'll end our days?
If we do not mend our ways
We've messed your world of green and blue
What are we supposed to do?
Don't you want to help us now?
Or is it that you don't know how?

80. THE GOOD AND THE BAD.

Playing as children
At robbers and cops
Fighting the bad
The good came out tops
We dreamed of being soldiers
And going to war
We dreamed of the glory
Not of the gore
With bows and arrows
Or gun in hand
We'd kill of the baddies
Throughout our land
Killing meant nothing
As only bad died
Day after day
The good men survived
As we grew up
We changed our games
Different ideals
Different aims
And now I'm much older
The killing goes on
But that's not my hand
That's now on the gun
Reality now is
Anyone dies
The good or the bad
Women or guys.

81. WHY?

I didn't ask, I didn't say
Perhaps it had to be this way.
Your funny laugh, that charming smile
Captured me for just a while.
A gentle touch, a warm embrace
The look of love upon your face.
Things you do, the way you walk
Even just to hear you talk.
Knocked by love on to the floor
In love with you
For ever more

82. FRIENDSHIP.

The years may slowly progress
And through them there has been
A friendship to be cherished
One that will remain.
So near you've always seemed to be
Although we're miles apart
And all the things you mean to me
I hold dear to my heart.
There if I may need you
Here if you should call,
Around to lift our spirits up
Whenever they may fall.
And as the years go slowly past
You'll always be to me
The same true friend you've always been
A friendship that will last.

83. ONE, TWO, THREE, ONE, TWO, THREE.

Round and round, round and round
Cascading violins
Creating a sound
That is magically musical
Sounds to the ear
Beautiful music
For all to hear
Building up loud
From a quiet beginning
Getting faster and faster
While dancers are spinning
To cascading violins
Creating the sound
Of a waltz
That is going
Around and around
                    Around and around.

84. TUNISIA.

A hot and noisy dusty sight
Fills the air from morn 'til night
Traffic rushing all around
Adding to this world of sound.

Beggars, rich men, rubbing shoulder
Some are young men, others older
A cheery smile, a friendly wave
Greeting all from birth to grave.

A place where many nations meet
And buy from sellers on the street,
A place to sit and watch the world
And life's rich tapestry unfold.

Streets of grit and streets of grime
Buildings looking old as time,
And people here are all the same
With 'friend' as their middle name.

Where 'ere you're from or going to
It's all the same to me and you,
But to these people in the sun
They've time to give to everyone.

No one need be alone
When traveling away from home,
This place that's full of noise and grime
Will make all welcome, every time.

85. PROMENADE DAYS.

Who are you?
What are they?
They promenade past
Every day.
Sometimes
On their own
Often
In a crowd.
Talking
In a whisper
Talking
Out quite loud,
Slowly dragging
Sometimes rushing
Standing back
Others pushing,
People, people
Everywhere
Promenading
Every day,
Who are you?
What are they?
People
On their holiday.

86. THE OLD SONGS.

The melodies still linger
Tunes of long ago
Songs to which we'd sing along
The words we all would know
Everybody joining in
It lifted spirits high
They don't write songs like that no more
Those songs of days gone by.

87. WHO'S NEXT?

Who can we trust
In the world today
When a bomb may be only
A person away
Without a warning
Striking out
Destroying our faith
Raising doubt
There seems no reason
To what they do
Killing themselves
To kill others too
Striking terror
Striking fear
Never knowing
If they're near
Will it be me?
Will it be you?
Or will they kill
Someone we knew?

88. AUTUMN.

The autumn leaves have turned to gold
Now the year is growing old
The weather starts to feeling cold
Now that autumn's here.

The autumn leaves fall to the ground
Silently without a sound
And very soon we're winter bound
Now that autumn's here.

The winds that blow the leaves about
Bring an autumn chill
And very soon the winter air
Will soon be cold and still
Now that autumn's here.

89. PLEASE YOURSELF.

Don't stand so close
To the edge of life
To keep them satisfied,
Don't sail as close
To the wind next time
They only run and hide.
You'll face the wrath
Of life alone,
No matter how you choose,
But choose to stand
Alone next time
Unless you want to lose.

90. PASSING PEOPLE.

It's sad but it's true
That people I knew
Are slowly passing away
And those faces I see
Now looking at me
Really don't know what to say
Thoughts of the past
And times gone so fast
Tomorrow too soon is today
Those people I knew
When their lives are through
In memories, with me will stay.

91. TOGETHER – YOU AND ME.

What a pity
What a shame
No one seems to take the blame,
All the sorrow
All the pain
When will peace come back again,
Some will kill
Some will die
Before they look you in the eye,
Here today
Gone tomorrow
Fills our lives with hurt and sorrow,
Given time
Day by day
Perhaps some time we'll find a way,
To live in peace
And harmony
All together you and me.

92. TRUE LOVE.

For the first time in my life I knew
The meaning of true love
My heart was shot by cupids arrow
A bolt from up above.
It happened on that first time
Our two hearts beat as one
And love has kept on growing
Getting ever strong.
I know that you won't leave me
That we will never part
For if you ever left me
You'd leave a broken heart.
And what good is a broken heart
To a lonely man
I'll love you through eternity
The only way I can.

93. ALL I HAVE TO GIVE YOU.

All I have to give you
Is a little of my love
I cannot give you falling stars
Or the moon above.
I'll lay my life before you
My heart, my soul, my all
I'll always be around for you
Just in case you fall.
And if my little piece of love
Is just enough for you
Take it gently in your heart
To last your whole life through.

94. SHARING.

The pounding on a sea shore
The beating of great wings
The ripple of a gentle brook
The bleating of the lambs

A few of life's great pleasures
That I have shared with you
As we travel down life's highway
I know you like them too.

We share so many good things
We also share the bad
We laugh as one when happy
We cry as one when sad.

The love of someone special
Is one more joy I've known
You've shared with no one else in life
Just saved for me alone.

95. THOUGHTS FROM A TRAVEL COURIER.

"This is wrong, and this ain't right
Can you fix the food tonight?"
"Could we change our room today?
The view keeps getting in my way."
"Could we change our room tonight?
We're kept awake by bright moonlight."
Where are all these people from
Why do they bother me?
I wish they'd go out for a walk
Or sit down by the sea.
"This ain't right and this is wrong
The drains are making quite a pong!"
"My bed's too hard I cannot sleep
It really makes me want to weep"
"The sheets are rough they hurt my skin
I really feel I can't get in"
Why do these people bother me
Where do they all come from?
Tourist season starts again
And just goes on and on.
"This is wrong and this ain't right"
Nothing suits the guests tonight
Complaints and moans are all they say
And nothing suits the guests each day.
"Can you fix the T.V. please?"
"My water's running slow"
Oh how I wish for Wednesday
When all these tourists go!

96. 'TIS THE SEASON TO BE JOLLY!

The festive season once more's here,
Lot's of wine and lot's of beer,
Loads to eat and more to drink,
That's when I begin to think,
Why'd we do it, what's it for,
Isn't Christmas such a bore,
Gaining inches, gaining weight,
Spending money - oops too late,
The overdraft just got worse,
It feels there really is a curse,
With gifts to buy and cards to send,
When will all this spending end,
If only I could hide away,
And come out after Christmas day,
With all the hassle finally done,
And Christmas day really gone,
With Santa well upon his way,
Riding off upon his sleigh,
And with the New Year finally here,
Once more I'm filled up with good cheer.

97. CHRISTMAS

They talk about snow at Christmas
Something 'bout peace on Earth
I know if there's snow
Outside we'll all go
For some jolly good fun and mirth.
There'll be Frosty the snowman and Rudolph
And Santa will be on his sleigh
I know if there's snow
And cold winds that blow
It will feel like a real Christmas Day.
There'll be turkey, stuffing and pudding
Plenty of food and wine
I know if there's snow
Mulled wine will flow
And we'll all get drunk in time.
They talk about snow at Christmas
But all we get is rain
Forget about Bing
That song he would sing
Over and over again.
Christmas seems to start early
Halfway through the year
The shopping to do
For me and for you
Thank goodness the day is now here.

98. BECAUSE OF YOU.

Above the clouds
My spirit soars,
Across the seas,
Along the shores.
Of feeling free
Or feeling bound,
Because of you
My love has found,
The feelings never felt before
And wants to feel for ever more.

99. YOU'LL NEVER WALK ALONE.

Do you look over your shoulder
When you think there's somebody there
Only to find when you look back
Behind you is empty and bare.

Do you ever hear following footsteps
Behind you in the dark
And when you turn and look back
There's nobody in the park.

Do you ever hear whispering voices
Quietly in your ear
And when you stop and look around
There's nobody standing near.

Do you ever feel sad and lonely
And wish somebody had shown
Although you may feel all of these things
You'll never walk alone.

100. THE DOLLY SISTERS.

There's Lollita and Francesca,
And my name is Collette,
We're the newest "Dolly Sisters"
A big hit you can bet.
We're out here on our hols
Taking time off in the sun,
Making sure we're eating well
And having lot's of fun.
Lollita is a lively one
And trouble now and then,
We have to watch her carefully
Especially round men!
When she sees a nice one
She'd chase him if she could,
But when you finally reach our age
You're legs just ain't that good!
Francesca is a quiet one
We have to take great care,
One minute she is sitting down
The next she isn't there.
And when we end up finding her
She won't know what she's done,
But when you finally reach our age
That's something else that's gone.
And finally, there is myself
The youngest of the group,
I haven't time for mischief
I have to watch this troupe.
Someone has to do it
For if I wasn't there,
They'd end up causing trouble
And do you think they'd care?
We're the newest "Dolly Sisters"
Lolly, Fran and Me
We are the very best of friends
As anyone can see.
And when you finally reach our age
For Dolly Sisters three,
It really is important
To have friends just like we!

www.ingramcontent.com/pod-product-compliance
Ingram Content Group UK Ltd.
Pitfield, Milton Keynes, MK11 3LW, UK
UKHW021321180426
11947UKWH00015B/1370

9 780955 993114